Carol's Christmas

By Stephen Glenn Large

DEDICATION

To all those with absent friends this Christmas.

CONTENTS

FOREWORD
BY TONY DEVLIN

My first meeting with Stephen G Large was in Starbucks in Belfast City Centre. He had sent a round robin email draft of his first stage play, 'Carols Crismuss' to local theatre producers and as soon as I read it, I knew that it had Brassneck written all over it and that I needed to clinch a meeting with him and deliver our pitch before another company would nab him. In true comedian style, he turned up late and allowed me to pay for both our drinks with the promise that he'd get the next ones.

Within minutes of sitting down and sipping over a mocha and a skinny latte, I knew that our paths were meant to cross and that we were predestined to collaborate together and that Carols Crissmus was the obvious vehicle to do so. Stephens philosophy, artistic vision, outlook on life, humour, sarcasm and wit was so similar to mine that I decided to cut through the bullshit and tell him there and then, that I couldn't match financially what any other company could offer him. Thinking that would be the end of the meeting, I promptly added that what I could guarantee him would be my unwavering commitment to bringing this cracking wee piece of work of his from page to stage by Christmas of that year.

I sat nervously (without showing it) draining the latte as I waited on him to tell me to 'f**k off ya chancer'. 'I like you lad. You've balls. I've googled you and you get shit done and the work you do is right up my street. I think we'll be a great match' came the response. 'Magic, So we're on' I said? 'Well I'm in talks with another big producer from here so it's only fair that I speak with him first'. 'Balls' I thought and we finished up the meeting and went on our separate ways. What a waste of £3.50 on a mocha. A day later I opened my emails. 'Lad, I'd love Brassneck to do this show'! Yes!!!

And so we sat about making it happen. With investment from both the Arts Council and Belfast city council along with a commitment from The Balmoral Hotel in West Belfast and the Strand Arts Centre In East Belfast (reflecting both writer & producers respective communities), we were on it like a car bonnet!

We thought outside the box and cast two well-known local actors and three theatre virgins. Not amateur actors but three of the best young comedians from the local circuit. We couldn't afford another fee for the narrator character so decided to voice over it. 'Who will we ask'? 'What about Julian'? 'Assange'? 'Simmons'! One Brassneck email to UTV and we got him (for an undisclosed fee).

And so the stage was set. With an inspired original soundtrack by Pat Gribbin of local international band 'The Adventurers' fame and an acid trip audio visual experience from designer Conleth White, we were punching well above our weight.

Opening night in the Strand Arts Centre, December 2016. A packed house. Tickets as rare as an executive at Stormont. 8pm. Boom! The projector fails. Computers shut down. A disgruntled crowd wait 45 minutes while we anxiously try to salvage something. 'Just start the show will ye? I've a babysitter on an hourly rate'! Feck it, let's go without. Two terrifying hours later, a unanimous standing ovation! Relief! The week sold out as word spread to the west. The Balmoral hotel packed for Christmas week. Audiences loved it! Julian loved it! Comedians talking of becoming actors! Me talking of needing counselling. A complete success from a first time playwright who chose Brassneck on merit over money. The gamble had paid off.

A year has passed since that manic, wonderful and ultimately fulfilling experience and although we're both doing other things at the moment, we are simply biding our time (Brassneck & Large) trying to figure out on what crazy, exciting and mad collaboration we can work on next... well if Carols Crissmus is anything to go by, it'll be even crazier and just as fulfilling as our first.

He never did buy me back that coffee...

WRITER'S NOTE

Thank you for purchasing this book, you have now officially ruined Christmas for yourself, forever. 'Carol's Christmas' was the first play I ever wrote, back in May 2016 - which I had hoped would go into production that December. Fortunately, Tony Devlin and his wonderful Brassneck Theatre Company decided to take a punt on an unknown writer when they made 'Carol's Christmas' their 2016 end of year production. The show opened 11th December in the Strand Arts Theatre, in my native East Belfast to a packed house. The cast consisted of one-liner king Sean Heggarty and his very talented, soon-to-be wife, Diona. Local stand-ups Paddy McDonnell and Ciaran Bartlett. Canadian-born Belfast actor Chris Patrick-Simpson and none other than Julian Simmons as our narrator. I cannot speak highly enough of the cast or of Tony and his crew, who brought this ridiculousness to life. I hope you enjoy!

ACT ONE – SCENE ONE
CAROL'S HOUSE

JULIAN SIMMONS
But now on the BRU TV, we have a real Christmas Cracker for ya's! Brassneck Theatre Company (aye Brassneck is right! You should see what they're paying me! I wouldn't normally get outta bed for less than a beg of sand) presents the world premiere, of wee Stevie Large's Belfast version of 'A Christmas Carol'! He's the man who puts the dick into Dickens! So strap yourselves in folks as you're in for a real festive feast! And now, without further ado ladies and gents, BRU TV brings you, Carol's Chris'mas...

Music: Scrooge Is Getting Worse - by Paul Williams, from the film, 'The Muppets Christmas Carol'. Song 'Mrs Scumbag' by Stephen G Large

CAST
Oh, there goes Mrs. Scumbag

Watch out and beware

If there's a prize for bein' a bitch, the winner would be her

Old Carol loves her money

And she's always looking more

If you can't afford to pay her, then the boys will knock your door!

There goes Mrs. Skinflint

She doesn't smile a lot

If you forget to pay the rent, she'll likely have you shot

She charges folks a fortune

For her higher interest loans

And if you miss a payment

Then the boys will break your bones

She must be so lonely

She must be so sad

She goes to extremes

To convince us she's bad

It could be a rouse or even a stunt

Actually - on second thoughts

She's just a horrible

... woman!

There goes Mrs. Loan Shark

There goes Mrs. Grim

She has no time for friends or fun

She'd quicker do you in!

Don't ask her for a fiver

Or a tenner on the strap

Unless you have a death wish

Or you're lookin' knee-capped!

There goes Mrs. Heartless

There goes Mrs. Cruel

She never gives, she only takes, yes that's her only rule

If bein' mean's a way of life

You practice and rehearse,

Then all that work is paying off

'Cause Carol is getting worse

Every day

In every way

Carol is getting worse!

JULIAN SIMMONS

Mickey Marley was dead to begin with. There is no doubt about that. The register of his burial was signed by the clergyman, the clerk and the undertaker. No, not yer big man outta the WWE!

Our Mickey was survived by his aul wife Carol. As well as being partners in marriage, they were partners in business. For years they were in the iron and steel business. She did the ironing; he did the stealing. After that, they set up a loan sharking business which they ruled the same way as they made love - with a clenched fist.

When our Mickey suddenly died on Christmas Eve fifteen years ago, Carol ran the business with the help of fella known as Bob Hatchet. Bob was the local hard man and he relied upon the collection jobs that Carol gave him in order to support his large wife and young family - I mean his young wife and large family! God forgive me!

On the morning in which this story begins, Carol is at her home with Bob Hatchet plotting the day ahead. Carol's nephew Rodney arrives but aul Carol welcomes Rodney with the same exuberance she would give to an aggressive yeast infection.

Carol is sitting at the kitchen table. Carol is eating a healthy cereal which she clearly isn't enjoying.

Bob Hatchet enters.

CAROL
You're late Bob.

BOB HATCHET
Sorry Carol. I nipped round to Cash Converters there to see if I could get my Krissy anythin' for Chris'mus,

CAROL
Well do it on your own time, not mine.

BOB HATCHET
I was looking for an engagement ring, so I was.

CAROL

Another one?? You've went through more rings than Sonic the fuckin' Hedgehog!

BOB HATCHET
You're a right grumpy ballix when you're on that diet Carol.

CAROL
I dunno how much more of it I can take.

BOB HATCHET
Anytime you wanna pack it in, just let me know. I'll gladly take that twenty quid off your hands!

CAROL
No. I'm determined to see it through this time. It feels like I've been on it forever though. How long's it been?

Bob checks his watch.

BOB HATCHET
Half an hour.

CAROL
Oh, all I can think about is a full soda. And a Twirl. And a tin of Coke.

BOB HATCHET
I've got something to take your mind off food.

Carol shields her eyes.

CAROL

Bob, you're not gonna show me that rash again are ye?

BOB HATCHET
No the penicillin cleared that right up.

CAROL
What is it then?

BOB HATCHET
Wee Bap McIlroy missed a payment on his loan.

Carol slams her fist into the table.

CAROL
That ginger wee bastard. Did you break his arm?

BOB HATCHET
No.

CAROL
Well what did you do?

BOB HATCHET
I had a word with him.

CAROL
Oh well that'll teach him!

BOB HATCHET
Carol, it's Christmas Eve.

CAROL
So what?

BOB HATCHET
If I broke his arm he wouldn't be able to work.

CAROL
I don't give a fuck if he's Santa - break his arm!

BOB HATCHET
But if he can't work then he won't be able to pay you back.

CAROL
You're gettin' sloppy Bob. People will be thinking we're going soft.

BOB HATCHET
But I thought -

CAROL
I don't pay you to think Bob. I pay you to bate ballix in. And when someone doesn't pay, then you bate those ballix right in. Do you understand?

BOB HATCHET
Yes Carol.

CAROL
My Mickey would be spinning in his grave, God rest his soul. He took no prisoners, let me tell ye. I remember some fella tried to stroke him a fiver.

BOB HATCHET
What happened?

CAROL
My Mickey broke both his arms – and that fella still managed to get his hole into work the next day!

BOB HATCHET
Really?

CAROL
Aye. But in fairness, the peelers said it was probably why he crashed the school bus.

Bob shakes his head.

CAROL
You can't give people an inch Bob. That's what my Mickey always said. And now he's gone it's up to me to uphold the Marley name. So it doesn't matter if they're a window cleaner or a gynecologist. You break their arms. Got it?

BOB HATCHET
Got it Carol.

CAROL
Now, what about that shop keeper who said he couldn't afford the protection money. Did you put a brick through his windies like I told ye?

BOB HATCHET
But Carol. It's Christmas.

CAROL
Then sing a fuckin' hymn while you do it.

Once again Bob shakes his head.

CAROL
And another thing. Make sure you're in early tomorrow. We've got plenty of collections still to make.

BOB HATCHET
Tomorrow? But -

Rodney enters holding a Christmas wreath.

RODNEY
Merry Christmas, Auntie Carol!

CAROL
Merry Crissmus my ballix.

RODNEY
Ah come on! Get into the Christmas spirit! It's a time to be happy.

CAROL
I don't know what you're so happy about? You haven't a light!

RODNEY
I don't know what you're so grumpy about? Sure you're loaded.

CAROL
So that's why you're here? You're looking a wee hand out?

RODNEY

Is that what you think?

CAROL
Well, you're just like all the rest of them at Chris'mus, aren't ye? Haven't got 2d to rub together but you'll be out spending thousands of pounds you can't afford on pointless shite no one needs.

RODNEY
But Auntie -

CAROL
Chris'mas? The same aul shite every year, so it is. Sitting in a living room watching Home Alone for the 400th time with all the people you try to avoid the other 364 days a year. Everyone wearing ridiculous jumpers and throwin' Quality Street down their fat necks.

RODNEY
But –

CAROL
... and a Brussel sprout fart-cloud hanging in the atmosphere like a layer of fuckin' smog.

RODNEY
Auntie!

CAROL
You can ding your bloody dong until it's merrily on high Rodney. Just leave me out of it. Cos I'd rather boil ma head.

RODNEY
I was hoping you'd spend Christmas with me and the family?

CAROL
Where's my pot?

RODNEY
Fine. Suit yourself. I'm sure the kids would love to spend some time with their great-auntie. Plus, I hate the thought of you all alone on Christmas Day.

CAROL
Me and Bob have to make a few collections tomara, so I won't be on my own – if that eases your conscience any?

RODNEY
My conscience is clear Auntie. I've always invited you to come and spend time with us. We've always made you feel welcome!

Carol lifts heaped tablespoons of the healthy cereal she seems repulsed by, before letting the contents slide back into the bowl.

RODNEY
What's that you're eating?

CAROL
Muesli.

RODNEY
I've never tried it. What's it like?

CAROL
Like falling face-first into a bucket of squirrel shite with your mouth open.

Suddenly there is a knock at the door.

CAROL
Answer that Bob, would ye?

Bob Hatchet answers it. A charity worker enters carrying a clipboard and pen. There are two things that Carol hates the most: giving money away and people looking for charity.

CHARITY WORKER
And how are we all doing this fine morning?

CAROL
Before you start your shite, whatever it is you're trying to flog, I'm not interested.

CHARITY WORKER
I'm not trying to sell anything madam. I am collecting for the homeless who suffer greatly at this time of year. A problem that could be solved if we all gave a little.

CAROL
What about the hostels? Is that not what our taxes are for? If I paid any *(winks to audience)*.

CHARITY WORKER
There are limited spaces at the hostels I'm afraid. Those who are left out would give anything to spend the night in a nice warm house like this.

CAROL
Would they, aye? And how many of them are you putting up in your own house Mother Theresa?

CHARITY WORKER
I still live at home with my parents or else I would.

CAROL
Still at home? What age are ye love?

CHARITY WORKER
Twenty-two.

CAROL
Twenty-two years of age and still suckling off your ma's diddy? I remember reading that your children should move out the moment they turn sixteen.

CHARITY WORKER
Really? Where was that?

CAROL
My ma wrote it in my sixteenth birthday card.

RODNEY
Well I set a direct debit up for the same cause a few weeks ago. It's only £5 a month!

CAROL
Did ye aye? I'm beginning to think you're f'n homeless you've been here that long!

RODNEY
Don't worry, I get the hint. *(stops with a thought.)* Are you sure you don't want to have dinner with me and Emma tomorrow? Her aunt Sadie will be there. She's about your age. I think you met her once before.

CAROL
Aye and her face tripped her the whole time!

RODNEY
It was her husband's funeral!

CAROL
Look I'm not going and that's final.

RODNEY
Ah, what's the point? *(Rodney hangs his wreath)* Merry Christmas Bob!

HATCHET
Merry Chris'mus Rodney!

CAROL
Merry ballix.

A visibly frustrated Rodney leaves Carol's house, most likely before he says something which he might regret. You get the sense that Rodney's annual pilgrimage to Carol's takes its toll on him but he refuses to give up on his cantankerous old aunt. Carol watches Rodney exit and then she rounds upon her other unwelcome guest.

CAROL
Are you still here? Persistent wee shite aren't ye? Look, you can give them this if you want?

Carol points at a huge cardboard box in the corner of the room with a picture of a 50-inch TV on the front of it.

CHARITY WORKER
That's awfully kind of you. But what would a homeless person do with a tv?

Carol laughs hysterically at the naivety of the young girl.

CAROL
Give away a brand new 50-inch TV? Are ye buckin' mawd? The TV is for me. They can have the box to sleep in if they want?

The charity worker doesn't dignify Carol's offer with a response. She storms out of Carol's home visibly upset. Carol is about to slam the door behind her when she hears someone singing so badly, it could be considered hostile.

HOODED TEEN
Halloween's coming on and the goose is getting fat... *(sings)*

CAROL
Wrong holiday ya buck eejit ye!

HOODED TEEN
Huh?

CAROL
What do ya want?

HOODED TEEN
Any odds Mrs?

CAROL
F' away off round our own door!

Carol grabs the wreath that Rodney had hung on her door and throws it at the teen as if it were a discus. The Teen tries in vain to run away but the wreath hits him in the back of the head and he lands face first into the snow.

HOODED TEEN
Here Mrs. You coulda give me brain damage or something! *(spits out a mouthful of snow)*

CAROL
You'd need a brain first. And just be thankful that snow's not yella!

Carol closes the door all the while chuckling to herself. She looks across at Bob Hatchet as if to share the joke with him but he looks glum.

CAROL
What's wrong with you? You've bake longer than Bruce Forsythe on the MDMA?

BOB HATCHET
She'll kill me if I say I'm working tomorrow.

CAROL
Jaysus. You can tell who wears the tracksuit bottoms in that relationship.

BOB HATCHET
Please can I have the day off Carol?

CAROL
People will think I'm going a bit soft in the head. But Christmas Day is grim enough without having to look at your aul sour bake. So you can take the day ya chancer ye. But I want you in all the earlier the next day!

BOB HATCHET
Thanks Carol. Merry Chris'mus

Bob Hatchet sprints off into the bleak winter's day before his employer has time to change her mind.

CAROL
Merry ballix!

ACT ONE – SCENE TWO
CAROL'S BEDROOM

JULIAN SIMMONS
That evening, our Carol went to her local and sat in the booth which she used to share with her late husband and drinking partner, Mickey Marley. After tankin' eight pints of Stella and a mixed kebab, Carol staggered home, before collapsing into her favourite armchair in a drunken stupor. After a while, the bell on the old grandfather clock tolled twelve times and each clang felt like a hammer blow to Carol's head.

Carol clutches her stomach.

CAROL
That F'n kebab.

JULIAN SIMMONS
As the bells chimed, another noise grabbed aul Carol's attention.

Clanking chains.

CAROL
It sounds like B A Baracus and Jimmy Savile are doing the Hokey Cokey out there!

Suddenly before her eyes, a ghost appears which Carol recognizes even if her mind forbids her to do so. The spectre is a tall imposing figure, wearing hundreds of fake gold necklaces which put a visible strain on his posture. Carol sits paralyzed with fear in her armchair.

MICKEY MARLEY
Carol

The sound of the phantom's voice makes Carol leap from the chair and cower behind it.

CAROL
Who's there? My husband is upstairs - he's a black belt in, in origami...

MICKEY MARLEY
Carol it's me, Mickey. Your husband.

CAROL
Mickey's been dead fifteen years to the day. Who is it? I'll have your knees done if you don't fuck off...

MICKEY MARLEY

You don't believe me?

CAROL
No.

MICKEY MARLEY
How could I prove it to you?

CAROL
Ok. What was our anniversary?

MICKEY MARLEY
14th April.

CAROL
No the 18th June ya bastard ye. Jaysus Christ it really is you! … No! I must be hallucinating. This happened before. I got a half & half with curry out of that stinkin' Chinese last year and about four hours later I could see giant iguanas crawling along the ceiling. You're just a bad dose of food poisoning. Aye, there's more chip & gravy than graveyard about you!

MICKEY MARLEY
Carol I want to warn you about the future.

CAROL
They're not making another series of Lesser Spotted Ulster are they?

MICKEY MARLEY
This is not a joke Carol! You see these gold chains? I forged these chains by the actions I made in my life. Every link was made by my greed. Now I must wear these chains for all eternity. Your chains Carol, are longer and heavier than mine.

CAROL
I'd look like a cross between Bet Lynch and Mr T! ... But you were only running a business!

MICKEY MARLEY
(Shouts) Can't you see what the cost of our business has been to me? It's cost me my soul for all eternity! We should've helped the local community - but instead we drove them even further into debt with our extortionate loans! We should've spread joy but instead we spread fear! I am here tonight to tell you that you have a chance of escaping my fate Carol!

CAROL
You don't see any of this on Ghost Hunters. I knew that Derek Acorah was fulla shite.

MICKEY MARLEY
Tonight you will be visited by three spirits.

CAROL
Well I hope to fuck it's gin, vodka and Vat 19, after this!

MICKEY MARLEY
Expect the first when the bell tolls one.

CAROL
Can they not all come at once? I'll be up all F'n night!

Mickey breaks his ghostly act and snaps at her, as if he was stood before her in the flesh.

MICKEY MARLEY
Yo! Are your ears painted on? When the bell tolls one, the first will appear. Listen to them. Your future depends on it Carol.

JULIAN SIMMONS
With that, Mickey Marley vanished as unexpectedly as he had appeared – and Carol was left alone on the earth for a second time by her husband.

CAROL
Merry Chris'mus? Merry ballix!

ACT ONE – SCENE THREE
CAROL'S BEDROOM

JULIAN SIMMONS
As Carol lay dozing on her favourite chair, the bell on the aul grandfather clock tolled once. Carol scanned the room for the presence of the ghost which aul Mickey spoke of. When she saw that the coast was clear, she afforded herself a little sigh of relief - and a fart.

Unfortunately for Carol, that relief was short-lived and suddenly the room was illuminated by a brilliant white light which temporarily blinded her. When she regained her sight, she was presented with the image of a grubby man with wild hair, in a suit -

Music: 'Day-O (Banana Boat Song)', Harry Belafonte

Carol's body no longer belongs to her. She begins to mime the words and actions to 'Day-O (Banana Boat Song).

BEETLEJUICE
Attention all shoppers!

CAROL
Are you the first ghost?

BEETLEJUICE
I'm the ghost with the most baby!

Beetlejuice laughs as though he smokes eighty Marlborough Reds per day, which triggers a coughing fit. He coughs something up and spits it into his inside pocket.

BEETLEJUICE
Save that for later.

CAROL
What's your name?

BEETLEJUICE
I'm guessing someone doesn't know the rules? Let's just call me the Spirit of Christmas Past, ok?

CAROL
Why are ya here?

BEETLEJUICE
Your welfare - and local fanny!

CAROL
Welfare? Oh Jaysus! Are you from the brew? Did some
F'er tout on me?

BEETLEJUICE
Not that welfare. Your welfare, as in your general well-
being. I'm here to ensure no harm comes to you in the
future, or some shit like that. Now, take a wing sister,
you and I are gonna jump through that window.

CAROL
Where? Out that windy? Sure I'd fall and break my neck.

BEETLEJUICE
(Shakespearean voice) Take thy hand and ye shall fly.

Carol takes Beetlejuice's hand which is fake and falls off. She gets a
fright and Beetlejuice belly laughs.

BEETLEJUICE
(Laughing) Gets 'em every time. Wait, hold on, what is it
you Belfast folk say? (terrible Belfast accent) Are you takin'
the hawnd outta me? (laughs) Come on, let's go!

CAROL
This will be the second recorded case of flying elephant
after Dumbo.

Beetlejuice extends his real hand and they stand on the window
ledge.

BEETLEJUICE

Remember to keep your arms and legs inside the vehicle! Now, let's turn on the juice and see what lets baby!

Carol took the spirit's hand and they passed through the window as if it wasn't there. They hurtle through the sky looking down upon the rooftops of Belfast. Before long the city disappeared and they are hovering above Carol's old primary school. As they came in to land, Carol can see the old school gates and upon closer inspection she realizes that they have gone right back to her own childhood. It's Christmas Eve afternoon many years ago when Carol was just a child. The sights and smell of white dog shite bring back a thousand memories long forgotten. A solitary child sits working at a school desk cutting a forlorn figure. They come in to land.

CAROL
Jaysus! That scared the shite right outta me.

BEETLEJUICE
Wooooo! That is why I won't do two shows a night anymore, I won't do it.

CAROL
Look! It's my old primary school! And it's me when I was a wee chile. Obviously my ma was still cutting my fringe with a hot poker at this stage. I look like Dave Hill from Slade!

Suddenly two schoolgirls enter the room and their way towards Carol whilst whispering and giggling.

CAROL
Quick! Hide before they see us!

BEETLEJUICE

Don't worry. These morons can't see us. Watch.

Beetlejuice starts jumping up and down in front of them.

BEETLEJUICE
Yo! Can you see a dead guy with green hair? Hello? *(to Carol)* You see?

SCHOOLGIRL #1
Why are you still here? The bell rang. It's the Christmas holidays!

CHILD CAROL
So.

SCHOOLGIRL #2
Aren't you excited?

CHILD CAROL
Not really.

SCHOOLGIRL #1
But what about all the presents? Oh, I just can't wait to open mine. What are you getting this year?

CHILD CAROL
I asked for a pair of roller boots but I'll not be getting my hopes up!

SCHOOLGIRL #1
How come?

CHILD CAROL

Last year I asked for a record player and I ended up with a tape-deck stolen out of someone's car?

SCHOOLGIRL #2
How'd you know it was stolen?

CHILD CAROL
Cos I was on lookout while my da broke into the car.

SCHOOLGIRL #1
Well Daddy's buying me the beach house this year.

CHILD CAROL
For Barbie?

SCHOOLGIRL #1
No, some real estate in California actually.

CHILD CAROL
Your da must be loaded.

SCHOOLGIRL #2
Well, Daddy said we have to make some cut-backs this year, so I'm not expecting another pony.

CHILD CAROL
What cut-backs?

SCHOOLGIRL #2
Daddy's had the waterfall feature ripped out of the 4th floor bathroom and we're down to three lobster based meals per day.

CHILD CAROL

God love yis *(sarcastically)*.

SCHOOLGIRL #2
Do you like lobster Carol?

CHILD CAROL
You're lucky if you getta fish finger samich sauce in our house. The closest anyone in our family's got to lobster is when my uncle Alfie had a dose of the crabs.

The two schoolgirls look at each other before bursting into fits of laughter. Child Carol is hurt by this but masks it admirably. The two girls concede that they aren't getting the desired rise out of Carol and they leave her alone again.

BEETLEJUICE
You guys must've been poor as fuck.

CAROL
You've no idea son. I remember one night two fellas broke into our house lookin' for money and my da said he'd give them a hand!

BEETLEJUICE
Ok! Fast forward!

Beetlejuice clicks fingers.

Carol and Beetlejuice remain in the same classroom which ages before their very eyes. The windows crack; bits of plaster fall from the ceiling; the furniture falls to pieces - and that's just the damage that Carol caused! There are signs that wee Carol has aged too. Her big pimply forehead has so many dots on it, she looks like the goalkeeper of the local darts team. Carol watches with great emotion as her younger self was joined by her older sister Fran.

FRAN
Carol!

TEENAGER CAROL
Fran!

BEETLEJUICE
Woah! What a piece of ass!

CAROL
I'll knock yer ballix in, that's my big sister!

Fran runs over to her younger sibling and administers a dead arm as her own unique way of conveying her affection. Young Carol rubs the sore area furiously but even the pain cannot quell her obvious delight at seeing her older sister.

FRAN
Come on, let's get home. We've got a big surprise waiting on you!

TEENAGER CAROL
A new TV?

FRAN
Our da just got out of prison!

TEENAGER CAROL
Prison? My ma said he was in the navy.

BEETLEJUICE

Trust me, the only water and seamen he seen was in the prison showers.

TEENAGER CAROL
I can't believe she lied to me!

FRAN
I can't believe you're so gullible!

TEENAGER CAROL
This is unbelievable! What did he go to prison for?

FRAN
Fraud.

TEENAGER CAROL
What'd he do?

FRAN
We were skint. So he wrote himself a cheque and tried to cash it.

TEENAGER CAROL
For how much?

FRAN
£200 billion.

TEENAGER CAROL
£200 billion? He could've tipped the whole planet into a recession if the bank had cashed it. Oh I'm pure scundered. Why can't he just make an honest living like everyone else's da?

FRAN
Here. Maybe this will cheer you up.

Fran hands Carol a vinyl Bay City Rollers LP which she hugs as if she were reunited with a long lost relative on Cilla Black's 'Surprise Surprise'.

TEENAGER CAROL
Oh my God! A Bay City Rollers LP! Amazing! Hold on – this must've cost a fortune. Where'd you get the money?

FRAN
I've been working a few extra shifts in the shop.

TEENAGER CAROL
Are you sure? Oh thank you!

They embrace.

BEETLEJUICE
She always was a giver.

CAROL
Aye.

BEETLEJUICE
She was generous too *(laughs)*

CAROL

Here ya dirty F'er! I'll break yer jaw! That's my sister you're talkin' about! She'd have given you her last she would. And look where it got her? Died without a bean to her name.

BEETLEJUICE
Wow, take it easy! I was just kidding. She had children too I think?

CAROL
Just the one. Rodney.

BEETLEJUICE
Your nephew.

CAROL
Aye.

BEETLEJUICE
You never bonded with him?

CAROL
He's like thrush.

BEETLEJUICE
Huh?

CAROL
He's an irritating c -

Beetlejuice puts his hand over Carol's mouth to stop her saying that vulgar word to describe a woman's genitals that rhymes with the fisherman Rex Hunt.

ACT ONE – SCENE FOUR
ROLLER DISCO

Carol and Beetlejuice walk through the classroom wall as though it isn't there and suddenly they appear in a local community centre, sometime in the past. Inside the hall, a 1970's roller disco is going on. The hall is illuminated by some lava lamp lighting equipment while a multitude of under-age drinkers skate around the perimeter of the room with all the balance and grace of a newborn foal. Carol appears overwhelmed by her nostalgia.

BEETLEJUICE
What are we on now? Like our third Christmas? I need to start seriously reconsidering my fee.

CAROL
I know this place!

BEETLEJUICE

Whoa! *(wafting)* It's not just the music that's funky in this joint.

CAROL
It's the Baxin' Night Roller Disco in the community centre. This is where I met my Mickey!

A young girl with the type of physique not designed for belly-tops, skates toward them at full speed.

CAROL
There's my wee mate Sylvia. A heart of gold but a bake like a stuntman's knee God love her!

Sylvia rolls over toward a young Carol who is stood speaking to another girl. Young Carol certainly isn't going to win any beauty pageants and her attempt at a Farrah Fawcett haircut makes her look more like Noel Edmonds. However, when stood beside Sylvia whose face would make an onion cry, her chances of snaring a male companion were significantly enhanced.

SYLVIA
Who are all these new fellas? It's like a sausage salad in here the nite!

CAROL
Bit of a girl as well. I think she thought knickers were ankle warmers.

BEETLEJUICE
Oh really? *(sprays breath freshener)*

CAROL

Keep it in yer stripey trunks you!

BEETLEJUICE
Hey! It's been like 600-years. You can't blame a guy for feeling a little anxious, if you know what I mean?

Sylvia drags across a boy who was standing on the periphery of the dancefloor and thrusts him into young Carol's path with a friendly thumping punch between the shoulder blades.

SYLVIA
Carol, this is Mickey. He says he works in waste management. Mickey, this is Carol.

YOUNG CAROL
Pleased to meet ye, Mickey.

MICKEY MARLEY
Aye, pleased to meet ye.

SYLVIA
I'll leave you two to it, then.

Young Carol and Mickey's attraction makes the situation palpable. They both search desperately for something to say that might end the deafening silence.

YOUNG CAROL
Do you smoke?

Mickey takes out a bag of glue and inhales.

MICKEY MARLEY

No thank you. I hear it's bad for ye.

Another soul destroying awkward pause ensues and Mickey begins to tug on the neck of his t-shirt as if to signal that he's warm.

MICKEY MARLEY
Phew! It's roastin' in here.

YOUNG CAROL
Aye.

Yet another awkward pause.

MICKEY MARLEY
D'ya wanna go outside for a bit of air?

YOUNG CAROL
Ok - but keep yer mits above the Equator big lawd.

Mickey offers young Carol his arm and they walk out of the community centre as though they were a courting couple strolling across a heath in a Jane Austin novel. Never mind that Mickey is high on glue and young Carol is a 15-year-old chain-smoker hoping to be groped. They stop outside and Carol sparks her cigarette.

YOUNG CAROL
It'd founder ye out here.

MICKEY MARLEY
Aye - it is pretty nippley - I mean nippy!

YOUNG CAROL

Well, I see the cowl weather has the opposite effect on fellas. It looks as though you're packin' a Walnut Whip down there.

MICKEY MARLEY
I've something that'll warm us up.

Mickey produces a hip flask. He takes a swig then offers it to Carol.

YOUNG CAROL
What's in that?

MICKEY MARLEY
Whiskey.

YOUNG CAROL
Where'd you get that from?

MICKEY MARLEY
I broke into my da's drinks cabinet.

YOUNG CAROL
Will he not go mental?

MICKEY MARLEY
Na. He helped me to do it. My ma hid the key again.

Mickey takes another swig. The potency of the drink makes him cough. He offers some to Carol once more.

YOUNG CAROL

No way. My ma's a snout on her like a police dog. She'll smell it a mile off!

MICKEY MARLEY
Don't tell me you're afraid of mummy shouting at you *(chuckles)*.

YOUNG CAROL
The shoutin' I can deal with. It's the slipper up the bake I'm worried about.

Mickey laughs.

YOUNG CAROL
I swear. She could skelp you up the head with a slipper from three hundred yards on a foggy day. It's like a rubbery heat seeking missile.

MICKEY MARLEY
You're a geg Carol. Go on. Just a wee taste.

Young Carol ponders.

YOUNG CAROL
Awk, alright. Just a wee sip.

Carol takes a sip and instantly spits it back out before coughing her lungs up.

YOUNG CAROL
That's rotten. It tastes like petrol.

A young male teen approaches. This is TUCKER.

TUCKER
Alright Carol, giviz a feg?

Without hesitating Young Carol reaches into her box of cigarettes and pulls one out. Tucker takes it out of her hand but before he can light it, Mickey grabs his wrist and twists his arm up his back.

TUCKER
AH! You're gonna break my arm ya header! See when you let me go, I'm gonna -

MICKEY MARLEY
You're gonna do what Tucker?

TUCKER
Mickey mate! I didn't know it was you! You keepin' well?

MICKEY MARLEY
What are you doin' spongin' fegs off this wee girl?

TUCKER
I'd just run out, I was gaspin' -

MICKEY MARLEY
If you need fegs, you come and see me like everyone else in school. Or are my da's Free State fegs not good enough for you?

TUCKER
Of course they are Mickey.

MICKEY MARLEY
Does my da not give a fair price?

TUCKER
Of course he does Mickey. I just heard two 11-year-olds say how they were able to smoke 40-a-day now because they're so cheap.

MICKEY MARLEY
If all that's true, then why are you out here pinchin' fegs off innocent young girls?

TUCKER Innocent?

Mickey twists Tuckers arm some more. Tucker yelps.

TUCKER
I'm sorry Mickey. It won't happen again Mickey.

MICKEY MARLEY
It better not. Don't forget, your ma gets fegs off my da too and he knows where you live.

Mickey releases Tucker from his grip, who immediately clutches his injured arm. Mickey then takes a wad of bank notes out of his pocket that would choke a Doberman. Young Carol is transfixed upon the money, an amount she's never seen before. Mickey slides one note out of the bundle and hands it to Tucker.

MICKEY MARLEY
Now go in there and get me and Carol two tins of Coke and two packets of Tudor Pickled Onion.

Tucker goes to walk off.

MICKEY MARLEY

And Tucker. Every penny of that change may survive the journey back here. Understand?

TUCKER
Yes Mickey.

Tucker exits. Even though Young Carol knows what she just witnessed was wrong she can't help but feel even more attracted to Mickey.

YOUNG CAROL
What'd you say your da worked in?

MICKEY MARLEY
Waste management. He just does the fegs and a few other wee things on the side to boost his wages.

YOUNG CAROL
Here, if you're lookin' a snog you may do it now. There's no way you're stickin' the tongue in after those pickled onion big lad.

They kiss.

BEETLEJUICE
Do you remember this chump?

CAROL
Remember him? I couldn't get rid of the F'er for the next thirty years.

BEETLEJUICE
But there did come a time when you had to part for good.

CAROL
I don't want to see it.

BEETLEJUICE
Don't worry. I brought tissues *(he produces a rolled up tissue from his pocket)*. Eh, don't use that one. It's a little crusty.

Beetlejuice clicks his fingers.

ACT ONE – SCENE FIVE
CAROL'S HOME

JULIAN SIMMONS
But now, take a look at thon dressed head-to-toe in black. I
don't know whether she's in mourning or she's about to
leave a box of Milk Tray somewhere. Some turn out aul
Mickey got, eh? Hardly surprising, he was about as popular
as Donald Trump at a Feminist convention.

*An eerie silence is occasionally interrupted by the clanging noises
coming from the old grandfather clock in the corner of the room. Carol
is dressed head to toe in black and sits on a dining chair alongside an
open coffin. She is the only mourner for the poor aul sinner in the
casket, her husband Mickey Marley.*

*Young Carol rises to her feet and walks across to the window where
she peers through the blinds.*

YOUNG CAROL
I definitely put 11 o'clock on the order of service. I wonder
what's keeping them?

Young Carol opens her front door and looks around before slamming the door back shut.

CAROL
Completely disrespectful. Imagine running late for a funeral.

Young Carol sits down again and fidgets for a few seconds.

BEETLEJUICE
Who are you kidding? Everyone else was in the pub celebrating!

CAROL
Ok, no one liked us. So what? When we knocked someone's door they'd pray it was a Jehovah's Witness. Popularity *(scoffs)*. It's like trying to catch butterflies in a jar. Who needs friends when you have money? Who needs people's love when you have their fear? Popular or not, people will never forget our name. We are Marleys and we did it our way.

Music: My Way - by Paul Anka

YOUNG CAROL
And now, you're dead my dear;

And I am here, alone and hurtin'

I wish, you were still here

To pour your stout, and tuck your shirt in.

You spent your whole life full

You pissed up each and every doorway

But more, much more than piss,

You did it your way.

Beetlejuice sprinkles some magic dust over the corpse inside the casket. Mickey Marley sits up as though he's a vampire in a Hammer Horror movie.

MICKEY MARLEY
Cigarettes, I smoked a few;

And that's what caused, my hypertension.

I helped out one or two

But not unless they paid protection

I never slept around;

Or threw my car keys into the ashtray,

But more, much more than this,

I did it my way.

CAROL
Yes, there were times, I fought with you

Like Ike and Tina used to do

I kicked your balls, I threw you out,

I clawed your bake and broke your snout.

You wanted back, I made you crawl;

We did it our way.

MICKEY MARLEY
And when, I punched that Spide

I must admit it was amusing

But then, he testified

I wore those gloves, to hide the bruising

And when, I found that tout

I kicked him up and down the driveway

And then I shot his knees

I did it my way.

CAROL & MICKEY
And when they said, that they'd forgot

To pay their bills, we had them shot

Now that you're gone I'll do the same

I will uphold the Marley name

The records show how much they owe

We'll do it our way!

BEETLEJUICE
Bravo, bravo. Well, my work here is done. I've got a recently deceased client at 3.30. I wonder who it is?

Enter JIMMY SAVILE, chomping on a cigar

JIMMY SAVILE
Now then, now then!

CAROL
What are you doin' with that aul disgusting creep?

BEETLEJUICE
Hey, we're like lawyers. Sometimes we don't get to pick our clients!

CAROL
I was talkin' to Jimmy!

JIMMY SAVILE
Well now guys & gals. I'm here for my haunting induction.

CAROL
You've some amount of chains Jimmy. Are they for your sins?

BEETLEJUICE
No. They're so the kids can hear him coming. Anyways, time for your nap Carol. Merry Christmas

Beetlejuice sprinkles some magic dust on Carol's head and she falls back into a chair asleep.

ACT TWO – SCENE ONE
CAROL'S HOUSE

JULIAN SIMMONS

Well, would ya look the state of thon, lyin' there with her tongue hanging out the side of her bake like an anesthetized Alsatian dog. She'd give ye the bile so she would. Even though she's been visited by two ghosts the night, Carol's still half cut on the Stella and probably thinks it's all been a dream. Well here, she's in for a shock so she is because the hauntin's not over yet let me tell ye! Speakin' of half cut, would you luk at the state of her up the back there. She had a 2ltr bottle of Diet Coke to her skull the whole way through the first Act. We all know it's fulla Barcardi ya mill beg!

Carol's beer and kebab induced coma is rudely ended when the old grandfather clock tolls twice. As the chimes bounce around Carol's skull, she peels her saliva encrusted face off the cushion beneath her and sits upright.

CAROL
I could ate the beard of Moses.

Carol takes out a bar of Diary Milk and begins to eat it. Suddenly, like what happened with the spirit before, a brilliant bright light fills the room and a silhouette of a tall well chiseled man appears. He approaches Carol from behind and drapes his muscular arms around her.

MUSIC: Unchained Melody, The Righteous Brothers

The spirit reaches over her and gently grasps the chocolate bar. Carol looks up at him. His hands dig into the chocolate. Their fingers seem to dance together. After a moment, she reaches up to him, her fingers covered in melted chocolate.

Suddenly, Carol spins around and to her complete and utter disbelief, she is presented with recently deceased Hollywood heartthrob Patrick Swayze. Carol proceeds to repeatedly slap her own face like a disobedient child's arse until she concedes that her eyes are not playing any tricks on her.

CAROL
Who the f' are you?

PATRICK SWAYZE
I am the ghost of Christmas present. Come Carol.

CAROL
Jaysus Christ the nite! It's Patrick Swayze?

PATRICK SWAYZE
Come forth.

CAROL
Get on yer back there big lawd and I'll come first, second, third AND fourth for ye!

PATRICK SWAYZE
Hurry Carol, we have much to see.

Conceding that Patrick would rather feed his feet into a wood chipper than come within a five-mile radius of her genitalia, a dejected Carol follows him.

CAROL
Alright Patrick, keep your braces on. I know I look more like Patrick Moore than Demi Moore but would it have killed ye to lumber me for five minutes?

PATRICK SWAYZE
Who's Patrick Moore?

CAROL
The astronomer, God rest his soul. He always had an eye for the stars. Fuck knows what the other one was looking for.

PATRICK SWAYZE
Take my hand Carol.

Carol gives him one hand then fans herself with the other, as she struggles to suppress her sexual urges toward the Hollywood hunk.

CAROL
Oh my baps are sweatin'! I wouldn't mind these hot flashes so much if they burned some of the fat off my arse!

PATRICK SWAYZE
You're trembling.

CAROL
Oh I wish my mammy could see me holding your hand Patrick. I remember taking her with me to see Dirty Dancing. She was like a dog in heat.

PATRICK SWAYZE
She was horny?

CAROL
No, I left her in the car and forgot to put a window down. By the time I got back she'd fainted.

They jump out the window.

Patrick Swayze leads Carol through a portal in her wall and on the other side they arrive outside the modest home of her hired muscle, Bob Hatchet. They pause just outside the front door and peer through the small living room window. Inside, Mrs. Hatchet is joined around the kitchen table by five of her six children; Kim, Kourtney, Khloe, Kylie and Kendall. Mrs. Hatchet is preparing the family Christmas dinner while her children lounge around with their heads buried in various devices such as tablets and smartphones.

CAROL
This is Bob Hatchet's house.

PATRICK SWAYZE
Wow! He sure does have a lot of kids.

CAROL
These are Bob's step-children, plus he has one child of his own. He's been married twice so he has.

PATRICK SWAYZE
Really?

CAROL
His first wife, Sylvia, left Bob with their son, wee Tim. And Bob ended up marrying Big Krissy Karwashian.

PATRICK SWAYZE
Karwashian?

CAROL
Aye. They're Romanian or somethin'. He adopted her five childer, Kim, Kourtney, Khloe, Kylie and Kendall. Between you and me, I heard that Kim one's a bit of a girl. She's had more willies in her than the Orange Order.

PATRICK
So why did Sylvia leave him?

CAROL
She got suspicious when Bob started making daily visits to a local car wash.

PATRICK SWAYZE
That does seem odd.

CAROL
Aye, especially when Bob couldn't fuckin' drive.

PATRICK SWAYZE
So, what happened?

CAROL
So one night Sylvia followed him. And there he was, in the back seat of a car with big Krissy. He was getting more than his gear stick polished, let me tell you.

PATRICK SWAYZE
Poor Sylvia.

CAROL
Don't worry about her. She married some well-off banker called Ben.

The Karwashians speak with Eastern European accents but use Belfast terminology.

KHLOE
Kim!

KIM
Sorry I'm late. Work was pure mental. Everyone seems to leave their shopping until the last minute.

MRS. KRISSY KARWASHIAN
I wonder what is keeping your da and wee Tim?

KIM
They probably stopped off for a couple of tins in the shebeen.

MRS. KRISSY KARWASHIAN
They better not have! I haven't been slaving over this microwave for the past five minutes for nothing! They will get my toe up their holes!

KYLIE
Can we stick one of the old Christmas home movies on while we wait on them?

Kylie, the youngest of Bob's daughters, rummages through some VHS tapes before lifting one out and reading aloud the label.

KYLIE
What's this one? Kim and Ray J?

Kim snatches it off her.

KIM
Oops! How did that get in there?

MRS. KRISSY KARWASHIAN
Sure what are you gonna watch it on? He sold the TV the useless bastard.

Mrs. Hatchet-Karwashian starts furiously sniffing.

KIM
Ma, what is it? You're sniffin' like a German Shepherd near Michaella McCollum's suitcase?

MRS. KRISSY KARWASHIAN
My fucking spuds are burnin'!

Mrs. Hatchet-Karwashian quickly waddles into the kitchen area in order to salvage the family dinner. Her daughter Kourtney is sat on a one-seater chair with her legs thrown over the arm while scrolling up and down Facebook. She momentarily deprives her smartphone of her full attention and notices something through the window.

KOURTNEY
My da and wee Tim are coming.

Moments later, Bob Hatchet and his only son, 'Wee Tim', almost fall through the door with their arms draped across each other's backs. Wee Tim is in his late teens and is a much smaller, thinner version of his father. He is clad head-to-toe in sportswear even though the only running he does is when being chased by the peelers. He is also carrying a crutch. Both of them are clearly shit-faced.

BOB HATCHET
Merry Crish-mussh *(slurring)*

MRS. KRISSY KARWASHIAN
I thought I told you not to come home drunk?

BOB HATCHET
Sure I had to come back - I've nowhere else to go!

Bob nudges Wee Tim and they both laugh uncontrollably. When they finally regain some semblance of composure, Wee Tim hobbles toward the kitchen table still clasping his crutch.

MRS. KRISSY KARWASHIAN
You can stop your acting now. You're not down at the brew anymore!

BOB HATCHET
Ah, leave him alone you. You should've seen him down there. Even I was convinced he couldn't work. With acting skills like that, he should be in a top television drama, like Hollyoaks or something. He must get it from me.

MRS. KRISSY KARWASHIAN
From you? You can't even act your age.

WEE TIM
Is dinner near ready ma? I'm starvin'.

MRS. KRISSY KARWASHIAN
You're not starvin'! Those poor wee childer in Africa, they're starving.

WEE TIM
Alright Bono, calm the beans!

Bob tries to pinch some food.

MRS. KRISSY KARWASHIAN
Keep your thieving hands off!

BOB HATCHET
So what'd you make?

MRS. KRISSY KARWASHIAN
Roast beef, ham, turkey, stuffing, sprouts, veg and I've done somethin' a little bit fancy with the spuds.

BOB HATCHET
Not burnt them black this time then?

Krissy slaps him. The children chuckle at the familiar scene of mild domestic violence.

MRS. KRISSY KARWASHIAN
Right everyone, sit down before it gets cold.

Before Mrs. Hatchet can finish her sentence, her family stampede towards the dining table; running in different directions and crashing into one another like wildebeest being chased by a lion in the Serengeti. Once they are all seated, Wee Tim lifts up a Christmas cracker and excitedly offers it around the table.

WEE TIM
Anyone fancy a go? I haven't pulled a cracker in about, um, it must be near a year?

BOB HATCHET
It's been longer than that son. I've seen some of the dogs sneaking out of your bedroom on a Sunday morning.

MRS. KRISSY KARWASHIAN
So Kim, how was the car wash today?

KIM
Busy ma. We washed 30 cars. 12 were BMWs.

Mrs Krissy Karwashian gets excited.

MRS. KRISSY KARWASHIAN
Oooh! What type were they?

KIM
The ones with the mobility stickers on them.

MRS. KRISSY KARWASHIAN
Your hands are blistered.

KIM
I know. I had to wash 15 cars on my own.

MRS. KRISSY KARWASHIAN
What about that young ginger boy I hired to help you?

KIM
Someone threw a brick through our window and shouted 'go home'. He thought they were talking about him and he took a half day.

MRS. KRISSY KARWASHIAN
The sons of bitches. That's the sixth window this week.

KIM
Don't worry ma. It won't be seven. None of them would do a full week's anything.

Wee Tim and Bob tug at the cracker. After a bit of a struggle, Wee Tim wins.

WEE TIM
Boom! Take that da!

BOB HATCHET
Shut up ya goat ye.

WEE TIM
Oh there's a joke, howl on and I'll read it. What did Adam say to Eve the day before Chris'mus?

BOB HATCHET
What?

WEE TIM
It's Christmas, Eve.

KOURTNEY
That's not even funny!

KIM
Feel wick for whoever wrote that.

Carol and Patrick stand and observe whilst the Hatchets tuck into their bountiful Iceland's Christmas feast. Despite their obvious flaws, the Hatchets seem to enjoy one another's company and present themselves as a tight unit. As Carol watches the dysfunctional family engage in festive frivolities, she realizes that something is missing from her own life and thinks of how badly she treated her nephew Rodney.

CAROL
The girls look as though they'll turn out ok but what about Wee Tim?

PATRICK SWAYZE
I understand that Wee Tim gets sent to juvenile prison for burglary and ends up on the streets - that's if his future remains unaltered of course.

CAROL
But what can I do about it? Sure it's not my fault?

PATRICK SWAYZE
Tim looks up to Bob. If you can somehow convince Bob of the error of both your ways, maybe Tim can break the cycle and be spared of this fate?

The sound of a can of lager being cracked open draws Carol's attention back to the Hatchets and their Christmas dinner. Suddenly, Bob hoists his tin of cheap Danish beer and requests that the rest of the family join him in making a toast.

BOB HATCHET
Raise your drinks, to Carol! The founder of the feast!

MRS. KRISSY KARWASHIAN
The founder of the feast *(spits on the floor)*? I didn't see that bearded hag in here slaving over a hot microwave?

BOB HATCHET
Come on love. Aul Carol pays my wages. She helps put grub on this table.

MRS. KRISSY KARWASHIAN
She was going to make you work Christmas Day the aul bitch!

BOB HATCHET
Anno but I ended up getting the day off. So relax love.

MRS. KRISSY KARWASHIAN
And she never even gave you a bonus this year. We had to pawn the TV.

Everyone, including Carol and Patrick, looks over at the old empty mahogany unit in the corner where the TV once sat. The Hatchet's faces are pained in such a way it's almost as if they're looking over at the ashes of deceased loved one - except for Bob, who looks suspiciously shifty.

BOB HATCHET
Sure it's all bloody repeats at Chris'mas anyway love.

WEE TIM
I thought you did get a bonus da? Sure you said that's what paid for all the drinks earlier?

Bob slaps Wee Tim around the head and Krissy repays Bob the compliment.

PATRICK SWAYZE
Come. We have more to see.

They are transported into a second home and into the middle of another festive family gathering. Rodney, his wife 'Big' Emma and several other couples, are in Rodney's living room. They are lashing the Pimms into themselves like there's no tomorrow.

RODNEY
And then she said that Christmas was a lot of aul b...
(pause) bum!

BIG EMMA
That aul doll would depress the life clean outta ye.

RODNEY
I seriously think she's depressed. Bipolar at the very least.

BIG EMMA
Na. Even they're happy half of the time.

RODNEY
I think she could use a short break or something?

BIG EMMA
Aye, hopefully a one-way trip to Switzerland.

RODNEY
You're hectic *(laughs)*.

GUEST 1
Sure why don't we play a wee game?

ALL
Let's play a game. No more songs. (Etc.)

RODNEY
I know one.

CAROL
Oh I love games!

Carol watches on with great enthusiasm and excitement. It is obvious from her demeanor that she has sorely missed the family interaction that she claimed to hate so much.

RODNEY
We'll play a wee game of "Guess Who?". I've got a cracker!

GUEST 1
Are you a man?

RODNEY
No

EMMA
So it's a woman

RODNEY
Duh, yes.

GUEST 1
Are you old?

RODNEY
Yes

GUEST 1
Are you popular?

RODNEY
Ha! No

EMMA
Are you generous?

RODNEY
No *(laughs)*.

GUEST 1
Are you in this room?

RODNEY
No

GUEST 1
Do you live in Belfast?

RODNEY
Yes.

EMMA
I know who it is!

RODNEY
Who is it?

EMMA
Your aunt Carol!

RODNEY
Yes!

Rodney and his guests laugh heartily, whilst Carol has the wind taken completely out of her sails once she realizes that they're laughing at her and not with her.

CAROL
I'll slap the chops clean off him…

RODNEY
What about a Christmas medley - a Bill Medley to be exact!

Music: (I've Had) The Time of My Life - Bill Medley and Jennifer Warnes

Big Emma and the rest of the guests become possessed and not in control of their bodies à la the dinner party in the movie Beetlejuice. They perform the dance routine from the final scene of Dirty Dancing.

Enter Patrick Swayze.

At the end of the routine Carol and Patrick attempt to recreate the famous lift but Carol charges into Patrick like a blind rhino and she ends up on top of him on the floor.

PATRICK SWAYZE
Carol, I don't know whether it's the music or the mulled Buckfast I had earlier but I think I want to take you up on that offer - if it still stands?

Carol has waited for this moment for just about her whole life. Sure, he's been dead seven years and is off his tits on tonic wine but it's still Patrick Swayze. The handsome spirit pulls Carol toward him with his manly hands which are clasping her shoulders. Carol closes her eyes.

CAROL
Oh my lips are twitching with anticipation *(turns to audience)* my mouth you dirty bastes!

Just as Patrick is about to stick the lips on her, Carol pulls away.

CAROL
Sorry Patrick.

PATRICK
What is it?

CAROL
Nobody puts our Mickey in the corner.

Carol slaps Patrick across the bake.

ACT TWO – SCENE TWO
CAROL'S BEDROOM

JULIAN SIMMONS
Once again, our Carol finds herself lying on top of her favourite chair but this time she is wide awake. Of all of the ghosts that she was due to be visited by that evening, Carol was pure shite-in herself about this one.

Carol sits up in her bed as the old clock tolls one. When she looks up, stood before her is the solemn Spirit of Christmas Future, in the form of Bruce Willis, from the movie The Sixth Sense. Although Carol considers Bruce to be a fine wee piece of ass, she does not feel the same warmth towards him as she did with Swayze.

CAROL
Ah Bruce Willis. I get it. 'I see dead people' and all that there aul shite.

Bruce Willis does not respond to Carol and instead he lights a cigarette using a Zippo lighter. He takes a draw from the cigarette and blows the smoke in her general direction. Carol looks petrified but persists in her attempts to coax a conversation out of him.

CAROL

Are you going to show me things that might happen in the future?

Once more Willis takes a draw from his cigarette and yet again refuses to engage her in conversation. His aloof behavior towards her begins to make Carol a little tetchy and she starts to overcome her fear of Willis.

CAROL

Come on Bruce big lawd. No need for the silent treatment, I'm bricking it as it is!

Bruce Willis lifts a hand and points onward, then drops his hand.

CAROL

Bruce you're about as sociable as a fart trapped inside a spacesuit son.

As before with the previous spirits, a vortex appears on Carol's bedroom wall and she steps inside whilst being closely followed by Bruce Willis. When they emerge, they find themselves standing outside a row of terraced houses where three women are gossiping inside a cramped badly maintained front garden. The women's voices are gravelly to the extent that they could sing bass for The Drifters and Carol cannot help but overhear their conversation.

BUSYBODY 1
Did you hear the biz? The aul bitch up the street died.

BUSYBODY 2
You're a liar? When?

BUSYBODY 1
Last night, so I hear.

BUSYBODY 3
I thought she'd never kick the bucket the miserable auld dog. She really was the tightest person in the whole of Belfast.

BUSYBODY 1
She was so tight she would only breathe in!

BUSYBODY 2
She was so tight, she found a plaster and cut herself!

BUSYBODY 3
She was so tight, she used to wake up in the middle of the night to see if she'd lost any sleep!

All of the busybodies laugh heartily.

BUSYBODY 3
Ah well, look on the Brightside. Looks like I don't owe her the money I borrowed for the sofa!

BUSYBODY 2
Or the money I borrowed for the chile's pram.

The three women cackle once again before dispersing and going their separate ways.

CAROL
I know some of those people Bruce. Are they talking about me?

Bruce Willis refuses to respond and instead he points in the direction of three tracksuit clad young men carrying some stolen goods across the street. Carol moves across to the other side of the road in order to eavesdrop on their conversation.

BURGLAR 1
Happy days our kid! We made an absolute killing tonight!

BURGLAR 2
Aye.

BURGLAR 3
What's your problem? You've just made the score of the century and you've a bake on ye like a Lurgan spade!

BURGLAR 2
It's Kaiser.

BURGLAR 1
Your Alsatian? What's wrong with him?

BURGLAR 2
He's getting very aggressive. I caught him on growling at the kids.

BURGLAR 3
In fairness, you'd be growling too if someone was sticking Lego up your hole!

BURGLAR 2
Anno. But I'm afraid of him snapping and biting one of them.

BURGLAR 1
Your da's always had big dogs. Why don't you ask him for advice?

BURGLAR 2
I already did. Fuck all good that did me.

BURGLAR 1
Why?

BURGLAR 2
He said he'd get his ballix off.

BURGLAR 3
What's wrong with that?

BURGLAR 2
Coz then I'd have an angry dog and a da with no ballix. How's that solve anything?

BURGLAR 1
No I think he meant - never mind. So what'd you grab?

BURGLAR 2
I got a laptop, a mobile phone and these sheets. They're still warm.

BURGLAR 3
You should keep those as a collector's item.

BURGLAR 2
How come?

BURGLAR 1
Cos it was the only warmth the aul battleaxe ever had!

CAROL
For F's sake Bruce! Talk about kicking a woman when she's down? Ok, I get it now. Everyone hates me. Please don't show me anymore.

ACT TWO – SCENE THREE
BOB HATCHET'S HOUSE

Mrs. Krissy Karwashian and her childer are in the family home together. Big Krissy is pouring herself a glass of ASDA Cava which was on offer for a fiver and is in quare form. She's conducting a little sing-song with the help of her children who also seem to be in good spirits.

Music: Ding Dong the Witch Is Dead, from The Wizard of Oz

MRS. KRISSY KARWASHIAN
Happy days! The bitch is dead.

KIM
Which aul bitch?

KOURTNEY
That aul bitch!

KHLOE
Happy days! The wicked bitch is dead!

Mrs. Hatchet rubs Kim's head as she dozes on the sofa and starts singing to her.

MRS. KRISSY KARWASHIAN
Wake up your sleepy head. Get your hole out of bed. Wake up, cos that aul bitch is dead.

KIM
Here's my da!

MRS. KRISSY KARWASHIAN
Right, stop the singing and pretend to be upset.

Carol appears to realize that this person whose death seems to be causing so much joy might be her own.

CAROL
Alright Bruce, I get the picture. They're all talking about me. This is what will happen to me unless I change my tune?

Bob Hatchet opens the front door looking quite despondent. He slumps himself down in his favourite armchair and puts his head in hands.

MRS. KRISSY KARWASHIAN
Well? Any change?

BOB HATCHET
Nope, she's still dead.

MRS. KRISSY KARWASHIAN
What are we going do for money now?

BOB HATCHET
Krissy, is that the only thing you can think of? The woman is dead.

MRS. KRISSY KARWASHIAN
I was just thinking out aloud. It's not as if doin' a few baitins' comes with a pension plan!

BOB HATCHET
I'll come up with something.

MRS. HATCHET-KARWASHIAN
Like what?

BOB HATCHET
Have I ever let this family down before?

Kim is clutching an iPhone and looking furious.

KYLIE
Da, there's a video of you on Facebook, dancing on a pool table with no trousers on. I'm pure scundered.

Bob takes a seat by himself.

CAROL
Bob seems to be the only one who gives a fiddler's fuck that this person is dead.

KIM
I think my da has staggered up from the Shebeen a little slower the past few weeks.

MRS. KRISSY KARWASHIAN
Bear in mind now, he hasn't got Wee Tim to keep him upright.

KIM
I miss Wee Tim mummy.

MRS. KRISSY KARWASHIAN
We all miss him very much but he'll be out soon. He shouldn't even be in there. It's a bloody disgrace so it is! He's been victimized because of his background.

Bob overhears this and rises to his feet.

BOB HATCHET
Victimized? He's been lifted more times than Dale Winton's shirt!

MRS. KRISSY KARWASHIAN
What about that time he got lifted and all he did was hold the door open for that young lady!

BOB HATCHET
She was in a changing room trying on a dress.

MRS. KRISSY KARWASHIAN
And the time he got arrested and all he did was nip out in the car for a few doughnuts with his mates!

BOB HATCHET
It's called joyriding love!

MRS. KRISSY KARWASHIAN
And that peeler who arrested him was a nasty piece of

work! Apparently, he even tried to get his own mother sent to jail!

BOB HATCHET
Where did you hear that?

MRS. KRISSY KARWASHIAN
It's true. His ma stuck his trousers through the wash with a £20 note in the pocket - he tried to have her done for money laundering!

BOB HATCHET
Awk away and shake your ballix!

MRS. KRISSY KARWASHIAN
It's true!

BOB HATCHET
Do you know who I saw today? Carol's nephew, Rodney. He was asking about you all and I told him our Tim was inside. He said he could maybe get Tim a job when he gets out.

MRS. KRISSY KARWASHIAN
How could he get him a job?

BOB HATCHET
Sure he's the new manager of the B&Q in Bangor!

MRS. KRISSY KARWASHIAN
Is there a B&Q in Bangor?

KIM
I dunno but it definitely starts with a B.

BOB HATCHET.
Aye, It only opened a few weeks ago.

MRS. KRISSY KARWASHIAN
I dunno if our Wee Tim would be fit for work. He has to take those valiums just so he can sleep all night.

BOB HATCHET
Well maybe if he didn't sleep all day, he wouldn't need them!

MRS. KRISSY KARWASHIAN
You're being too hard on him.

BOB HATCHET
No Krissy, we haven't been hard enough on him. Can't you see that all of this is our fault? Our son is in prison because of the poor example we have set for him. He's watched us lie and cheat and blag our way through life. I blame myself. He's just like me, my son is just like me...

Music: Cats In The Cradle - Harry Chapin - Cats in the Cradle, DLA Remix by Stephen G. Large

My chile arrived just the other day

But I said fuck that and I ran away

Now I've got letter from the CSA

And one from Jezza Kyle for a DNA.

And he was talkin' 'fore I knew it, and as he grew

He'd say "I'm gonna be like you, Dad

I'm gonna sign on the brew"

Well my da's in jail and my ma's a balloon

Is it any wonder that I'm on the brew

When you comin' home, Da

I don't know when, cos yer ma's movin in with Ben

Your ma's movin in with Ben

My son turned ten just the other day

I bought him twenty fegs and a milky way

'can you teach me how to smoke' I said 'Not today

I gotta thing at the brew and the DLA'

And as I walked away his smile it grew

He said, "I'm gonna be like you, yeah

Pretend I'm disabled too!'

Well my da's in jail and my ma's a balloon

Is it any wonder that I'm on the brew

When you comin' home, Da

I don't know when, cos yer ma's got engaged to Ben

Your ma's got engaged to Ben

I hadn't seen my son in about a year

He was sent to Maghaberry for dealing gear

I said, "I'd like to see you if you don't mind"

He said, "I'd love to, Dad, do you wanna line?'

You see my girlfriends a melter and her kids are too

Sure I'll see you down at the brew, Dad, I'll see you down at the bru

And as I hung up the phone it occurred to me

He'd grown up just like me

My boy was a lazy B

Well my da's in jail and my ma's a balloon

Is it any wonder that I'm on the brew

When you comin' home, Da

I don't know when, cos yer ma's up the duff by Ben

Your ma's up the duff by Ben

JULIAN SIMMONS
Aul Carol and Bruce arrive at an eerie old graveyard. It'd give ye the willies. Bruce leads the way with Carol wrapped around him like koala bear hugging a tree. Suddenly they come to a halt and once again Bruce extends his pointed finger towards something in the distance.

CAROL
Bruce, the dead person that no one cares about, is it me?

As the mist momentarily subsides it becomes clear that the spirit has been directing Carol towards a tombstone. She is afraid to look because she knows that this unfortunate soul's gravestone might be her own.

CAROL
Whose grave is this?

The spirit reiterates his instruction by pointing towards the old memorial. Carol resigns herself to the fact that she will have to face her own mortality.

CAROL

Before I look at it, please tell that these are things that I can change?

Bruce Willis points down towards the grave.

CAROL

Awk for fuck sake Bruce, speak to me! This is even more awkward than that interview you did with The One Show.

Carol kneels before the monument and clears some branches to reveal her own name. She breaks down and begins to sob.

CAROL

No... Carol Marley! Jaysus Christ la night!

Bruce Willis leaves Carol slumped over her grave. She looks up to the heavens and pleads for a shot at redemption.

CAROL

Oh sweet Mary and Joseph. Oh baby Jesus! Sweet 8lb 6 baby Jesus! Please give an aul sinner a chance to turn her life around. I promise that I'll change my ways. I'll even stop taking change back from the collection plate. Just give me one more shot at life and I'll show you how generous and kind I can be. When you took our Mickey near Christmas time, I couldn't bear to celebrate it. But I swear to you, I shall ding every single dong that's merrily on high if you just give me a chance!

ACT TWO – SCENE FOUR
CAROL'S HOUSE

JULIAN SIMMONS

And so, for the final time that day, aul Carol found herself on her aul seat. However, unlike the other times when she was pure shite-in a brick, Carol was all biz with herself. Probably because she wasn't six foot under the ground. She hopped off the bed and performed a two-step shuffle in sheer ecstasy. She realized that her prayers had not fallen upon deaf ears and the big 'lawd' upstairs had given her another bite at the cherry!

CAROL

I'm alive! I'm alive!

Carol glided across the room whilst performing a merry jig. She decided to go out into the street and share her reinvigorated lust for life with others. However, such was her giddy frame of mind at the time, she committed the greatest fashion faux pas Belfast had ever witnessed by putting on her old duffle coat and Crocs before heading out the door. She exited her front door and then threw her hands up into the air triumphantly.

CAROL

I don't know what to do! My wee head's as light as a feather. I am as horny as a school-boy. I feel like I'm pished! How long have I been dreaming for?

The Hooded Teen that Carol had scalped up the head with a Christmas wreath the day before walks past her door. The teen notices Carol then starts to run unsuccessfully in the snow, before landing in a heap at her feet.

CAROL
Yeo! What's today?

HOODED TEEN
Wha?

CAROL
What day is it?

HOODED TEEN
Are you on the workman's glue or somethin' love? It's Crissmus Day?

CAROL
(To herself) It's Crissmus Day! I haven't missed it. Patrick Swayze and Bruce Willis did me all in one night!

HOODED TEEN
Definitely on the glue love!

CAROL
Do you know if the Cash Converters around the corner is

still open?

HOODED TEEN
Aye. I'm only after pawning my Playstation so I can go out on Baxin Night. Then I'll buy it back on Monday once I shift this gear.

CAROL
See the TV in the window? Go and get me it and I'll give you a score note.

HOODED TEEN
Make it £25.

CAROL
Yo! I've been haunted – I haven't gone fuckin' mental!

HOODED TEEN
Carry your own TV then -

CAROL
OK, ya chancer. Here's the money. And don't even think about stealin' it. I know where you live!

HOODED TEEN
Are you up to your neck or something?

CAROL
No, I used to work for Royal Mail. Of course I'm up to ma neck. Now hurry up!!

The hooded teen runs off in search of the TV to secure his £25 reward fee and immunity from a potential hiding. Simultaneously, the charitable worker whom Carol had offended so deeply the previous morning crossed their path. Before she could get offside, Carol made a point of grabbing her attention.

CAROL
Merry Christmas young lady!

CHARITY WORKER
Mrs. Marley?

CAROL
Yes! Same name but a very different person love, I assure you! I've had a wee think about what you said and I wanna help!

CHARITY WORKER
That's great! Have you got your bank details handy?

CAROL
No sod that! I've got a better idea. I've got two spare bedrooms in that aul house of mine. Plenty of room for some of the homeless folk during these bitter winter months. Just tell them to bring ear plugs. I snore like a bastard.

CHARITY WORKER
Yes... of course. Please take this. You're only half dressed!

The charity worker takes a scarf from around her own neck and hands it to Carol. Although the scarf was green and Carol hated green, she becomes quiet emotional at the gesture and hugs the young girl.

CAROL
Thank you. Merry Christmas and God bless love!

Suddenly, as if by some clumsy plot twist, Carol's nephew Rodney comes along. Rodney looks on in total disbelief as his jovial aunt hugs the charity worker she verbally assaulted in his presence a matter of hours before.

RODNEY
Auntie Carol?

CAROL
Rodney!

Carol runs over and embraces an utterly bewildered Rodney.

CAROL
Merry Christmas nephew! Am I still welcome at dinner today? I really haven't spent enough time with your lovely wife and kids. What about wee Sadie? Is she there? She's quare craic so she is!

RODNEY
Y-yes...of course. We'd be delighted to have you!

CAROL
Good! I'll be round shortly love, I've just got one more thing to take care of!

Carol kisses Rodney on the cheek and skips down the road. Rodney's not sure what has caused this sudden and inconceivable transformation in his dear aunt and if the truth be told he doesn't care. For even if this is merely a momentary lapse from her miserable existence, Rodney is determined to enjoy every last second of it.

ACT TWO – SCENE FIVE
BOB HATCHET'S HOUSE

JULIAN SIMMONS
Well here, hasn't the big girl fairly changed her tune? Sure she's giggling there like a Bloomfield 3rd year on laughing gas! But before she knocks Bob's door, she gets back into battle-axe mode...

Inside, the Hatchet-Karwashians are opening a few Christmas gifts and having a wonderful time. Carol composes herself with great effort and raps at their door as if she is on official business. Almost immediately the door is opened by a shocked and frightened looking Bob Hatchet holding a pair of novelty socks.

CAROL
(growling) Why didn't you show up for work this morning ya waster ye?

BOB HATCHET
Sure it's Crissmus? And you said I could have the day off?

CAROL
Are you on the Bucky again Bob? As if Carol Marley would give anyone the whole day off – even if it is bloody Chris'mas!

BOB HATCHET
But I could've swore that you said -

CAROL
Look ya wee ballix ye! I'm not going to listen to this tripe another second, and that's why *(she slaps Bob on the shoulder, nearly knocking him over)* I bought your old TV and I'm going to swap you it for my new one!

BOB HATCHET
What?? The 50 incher?

CAROL
Yes Bob, the fitty!

Upon hearing the news, Mrs. Krissy Karwashian faints in her chair while her children celebrate the news like people possessed.

CAROL
Where's Wee Tim?

WEE TIM
What's happ'nin' Carol?

CAROL
And for you son, I'm gonna make sure our Rodney gives you a job and keeps you out of bother!

WEE TIM
A job?

CAROL
No need to get emotional or thank me. You can start on Monday son!

Wee Tim drops to his knees on the spot and starts to cry. He's completely devastated at the thought of having to work for a living although Carol mistakes these for tears of joy.

CAROL
He's so happy he's crying. Awk God bless him.

BOB HATCHET
Carol how can I ever repay you?

CAROL
By gettin' your lazy hole into work tomorrow. You owe me a day Bob!

Well you didn't think I'd go completely soft did yas (to audience)? Merry bloody Christmas everybody!

JULIAN SIMMONS

And aul Carol was good to her word! She let those homeless people sleep in her own home and she even got wee Tim that job - even if he did go on the long term sick after two days! Some people were sceptical of the 'new Carol'. Some people even laughed. But Carol let them laugh because laughter was good for their hearts. And she never ate another kebab for the rest of her life.

(Looks at watch) Right, is that me done? Pamela Ballentine's havin' a full scale blitzer at hers la night and I hear wee Jamie Dornan's making an appearance *(big wink to audience)*. Merry Christmas everybody *(KISS)*.

Music: The Pogues - Fairy Tale of New York – DLA Remix – by Stephen G. Large

We've got Spars

Dodgy bars

Sovereign rings of fake gold

Where a mother of three

Is fifteen years old

You said that if I gave you

Half of my E

You'd buy me a

Subway 6inch with cheese

You weren't handsome

You weren't pretty

We were both off our diddies

When the DJ stopped playing

We chanted 'one more'

The more I kept drinking

The less you looked minging

I pissed round the corner

While you took a shite

The boys of the old She-been Choir

Were singing 'DLA'

And their balls were hanging out

On Christmas Day

You're scummy

You're a drunk

You've breath like a skunk

You haven't a tooth in your ugly big head!

You fat smelly bastard

You're hung like a hamster

Happy Christmas your ballix

Hope t'fuck it's your last!

The boys of the old She-been Choir

Were singing 'DLA'

And their balls were hanging out

On Christmas Day

I could have been someone

Aye fuckin' dead on

You've ruined my life ya B

Since I met you.

Let's go on holiday

I'll get a crisis loan

We'll do a feg run

Just don't tell the brew.

The boys of the old She-been Choir

Were singing 'DLA'

And their balls were hanging out on Christmas Day!

ABOUT THE AUTHOR

2016 saw the emergence of Stephen G Large as one of Northern Ireland's hottest new comedy writers. Founder of and sole contributor to the satirical Facebook page 'Dundonald Liberation Army', Stephen has amassed thirty-thousand online followers in the two years since its inception. The 35-year-old's self-published book of the same title stormed to the top of Amazon Kindle Download Charts within a week of its release in March of last year. He followed this up with his second publication in May 2017, 'A Dog DLA Afternoon', which peaked at #6 in the Kindle charts.